Everything Never Comes Your Way

Everything

Never Comes Your Way

poems

Nicole Stellon O'Donnell

Book design by Mark E. Cull

Library of Congress Cataloging-in-Publication Data

Names: O'Donnell, Nicole Stellon, author.
Title: Everything never comes your way : poems / Nicole Stellon O'Donnell.
Description: First edition. | Pasadena : Boreal Books, [2021]
Identifiers: LCCN 2021013425 (print) | LCCN 2021013426 (ebook) | ISBN
 9781597099240 (trade paperback) | ISBN 9781597099431 (epub)
Subjects: LCGFT: Poetry.
Classification: LCC PS3565.D597 E94 2021 (print) | LCC PS3565.D597
 (ebook) | DDC 811/.54—dc23
LC record available at https://lccn.loc.gov/2021013425
LC ebook record available at https://lccn.loc.gov/2021013426

The National Endowment for the Arts, the Los Angeles County Arts Commission, the Ahmanson Foundation, the Dwight Stuart Youth Fund, the Max Factor Family Foundation, the Pasadena Tournament of Roses Foundation, the Pasadena Arts & Culture Commission and the City of Pasadena Cultural Affairs Division, the City of Los Angeles Department of Cultural Affairs, the Audrey & Sydney Irmas Charitable Foundation, the Meta & George Rosenberg Foundation, the Albert and Elaine Borchard Foundation, the Adams Family Foundation, Amazon Literary Partnership, the Sam Francis Foundation, and the Mara W. Breech Foundation partially support Red Hen Press.

First Edition
Published by Boreal Books
an imprint of Red Hen Press
www.borealbooks.org
www.redhen.org

Printed in Canada

Acknowledgments

Thank you to the editors of the following literary magazines for giving these poems (or versions of these poems) their first homes:

Arcturus: "At St. Joseph of Cluny Higher Secondary School, Puducherry, India" and "On the Way to Kuyilapalayam Higher Secondary School, Puducherry, India"; *Bellingham Review*: "Lyric Confesses" and "Necessary Premises"; *Beloit Poetry Journal*: "Advice to the Young Right Fielder"; *Brevity*: "Seascape with Eagle, Driftwood, Ravens, Seagull, Two Men, and Their Phones"; *Dogwood*: "Canzone Basking in the Pre-Apocalypse"; *Fourteen Hills*: "Another Incomprehensible Poem"; *Los Angeles Review*: "Incomprehensible Manifesto"; *Passages North*: "Chicago Gothic"; *Prairie Schooner*: "Picking Cranberries" and "Picking Crowberries" (as "Picking"); *Redivider*: "Pluck the Strings without Delay"; *Watershed Review*: "A Reply to the Obtrusive Narrator"; and *Zyzzyva*: "A Matter of Fact."

"Winter, Moving Still" and "Winter Landscape with Flirting Tourists" were published as part of the artist-in-residence program at Denali National Park.

I acknowledge these words were composed on and about the unceded ancestral lands of the Ahtna, Dena'ina, Tanana, and Koyukon Dené peoples, and the Sugpiaq people, who stewarded these lands for thousands of years and continue to steward these lands today. I am grateful to live and work here.

Thank you to the National Park Service and Denali National Park for my time in residency in Denali. My reflections on nature writing, John Haines, and the relationship between the self and nature began while I stayed at the Savage River cabin. Thank you to Kim Arthur, David Bechkal, Denny Capps, Tara Lewandowski, Cass Ray, Susan Wright, and all of the Denali staff for sharing your knowledge and time with me.

Thank you to the Rasmuson Foundation for the support of an Artist Fellowship and to the Alaska Arts and Culture Foundation for the support of a Connie Boochever Fellowship for Emerging Artists and an Alaska Literary Award. Their generous gifts provided me with the time to write these poems.

I am also grateful to the US State Department, the United States–India Educational Foundation, and the Fulbright Foundation for the support of a Fulbright Distinguished Award in Teaching, which allowed me to travel in India and visit schools there. Rev. Fr. P. Paul Rajkumar, Philomena De Condappa, and the students of Pope John Paul II College of Education, I hold you in my heart always.

for Sarah

Contents

Everything Never Comes Your Way

Advice to the Young Right Fielder

Hold the glove to your face,
cupping your chin.
Peek through the holes
and the world will telescope out.

See your mother sitting in the stands.
See the pitcher swoop her fast arm.
Breathe in warm glove.

You have been put here
because you are good
at being wrong.

Be wrong well.

Catalog the dandelions,
the lumpy lawn,
the foul line's chalky trace,
the cloud that rises from first base.

Stand, unready,
in the green nothing
you have been allotted.
Close your eyes.
Don't worry.

Everything never
comes your way.

1

Leave Out the Hours

Memoir

Leave in bad breath, adult acne, ulcerative colitis. Leave out the hours you spend on the couch watching just one more episode. Confess to the affair and the drugs, but don't mention the murder. Never mention the murder, even though you think a court would call it manslaughter. Confess you cheated in school, but leave out the cancer scare in your midthirties that left you weeping in the rocking chair as you nursed your five-month-old to sleep. Everyone has that kind of story. Consider writing about the cancer that baby would get when she was eight. No, save that for its own book later on. But don't wait too long. Once she's a teenager, she won't want you writing about her cancer. Leave out tasting moose heart for the first time and spitting it on your plate. Leave in the inflated ptarmigan stomach. Leave out the fireflies, or leave them in. Leave out the ripped underpants, the banana peels, your mother lighting cigarettes on the stove. Wait, leave that in, but leave out the after-school cookies. Leave in the wine. Leave in the crash, the glass in your chin. Leave in that time you got caught deliberately losing at strip poker in middle school. That's the good kind of shame. Every reader wants a little cringe without much terror. Leave out college. Nobody wants to read that these days.

Emptiness

I know you are here, but nowhere I see. The Zen master calls us upstairs
one by one to his chamber for our interviews. No you on the stairs. My
head, a tangle of bother about the woman on the zafu across from me
who shifts every ten minutes. Chair to cushion, cushion to chair. Is that
allowed? Every forty minutes we circle the cushions. Is it not enough?
Why do I care? Legs asleep, knee aching, I think *who are these people I am
not-talking with? People I meet and not-meet.* Then I catch myself and label
the thought *thinking*. I slept on the floor near the deck door, or not-slept,
with all the bumbling to the bathroom in the middle of the night. The
hallway light off, then on, then off again. The whole night I waited for
nothing to show up. Nothing ever did.

At St. Joseph of Cluny Higher Secondary School, Puducherry, India

Because the teacher is reading aloud, because the morning is warm and the ceiling fans whisper a backbeat to her voice, because I sit among the children on the hard wood benches, because the room is a blue like a faded noon sky, because the words are soft in her throat and softer in my ears, I forget the seventy students who called out *Good Morning, ma'am* and *God Bless You* in welcome. I forget the chair scratch on concrete, the sweat, the shifting to give the guest a seat directly underneath the ceiling fan. I forget the notes I'm supposed to take about how she is teaching the poem. Only her voice, her pink-flowered sari, her posture, her the-teacher-is-reading-to-you lilt. Only the room full of fifth standard girls in plaid uniforms, all listening. Only the listening. Listening so strong that I shrink to my fourth-grade self, and when she asks, *Are we ready for the next stanza, children*, I almost say *Yes, ma'am*.

By Proxy

I don't know how you're doing this.
——the well-meaning people who don't know what to say

There is no not doing this.
My child is that child. Another bald child.
No eyelashes. No eyebrows.
We all know what that means.
You know. I know.
It means *the worst thing*
a parent can imagine.

Look at the pictures online:
One kid trails an IV.
Another sits in a bed
visiting with a football player.
A close-up: a small hand
crowned with a hospital bracelet
holds an adult's hand.

I would have volunteered, held
the pain in my body,
like I held her in my body
before she was born.
Pain might have squirmed
and turned, like she did
at eight months, making me
scared she'd be breech.

I have room for more scars. Please.
A diagonal slash
across my abdomen, a numb
triangle beneath the white line.
I have space. Give me
a port scar, a bubble

under my collarbone.
The lung biopsy scar,
a chip beneath
my shoulder blade.

If the only way out is through,
then pull me all the way through,
like a needle.
Let what little
I am allowed to offer
be a thread,
stitching this cut
through our lives
back together.

And you, dear one. You only say you
don't know how I am doing this
because you believe your relief
over not being me will protect you
from being me someday.

And me, I have imagined worse things.
I can't stop imagining worse things.
That's how I'm doing this.

Mothering Martha and Mary

Lord, don't you care that my sister has left me to do all the work by myself?
—Luke 10:38–42

Daughters are like that, bickering.
One has done something. The other did it first.
One steals the other's pants and swings them
over her head. The other screeches.
One demolishes the bedroom
while the other weeps in the top bunk.
The tears have something to do with Silly Putty.
One makes faces naked in the bathroom mirror
to prevent the other from brushing her teeth.
One punches the other in the face
while she is sitting on the toilet. Crying,
they tattle. Shouting, they tattle.
Jesus Christ, I say, knock it off.

Jesus Christ, I say,
you were wrong.
I saw Mary sitting there
at your feet,
blinking her lashes,
baiting her sister,
and you let her
get away with it.

When the Anarchist Shaved My Head

for Chris Allen

In his cabin the oil drip smell and log walls made their own climate. I sat
in the chipped metal chair from the dump. Like all punk rock boys he
had a cast iron pan and no girlfriend. He unfolded newspapers around
the chair. Through my jaw, I felt razor buzz. Through my smooth head,
I felt his rough hand. Afterward, he put my hair out on the snow, laying
clumps in a careful pattern, an offering for the animals. What use could I
have for it then?

Lonely Owl

Evenings
early and late
under the star-black sky
punctuated
by satellites
the boreal owl calls
from somewhere
in the aspen.
Five beats.
Not *who*,
but *whowhowhowhowho*,
meaning *Why am I still alone?*

His feathered loneliness,
was so much like yours
when you went out
to feed the chickens
and look at the stars,
and looked back to see me
through the living room window:
laptop open
face lit with green light,
so unaware of you,

you stood on the deck
hooting at me: five beats
copying the owl in his sadness
calling me outside to see
the aurora and stars
and breathe in the cold moment
with you.

I would love to say
I heard you,
but I didn't.

I never even looked up.

Scan Day

The pediatric oncologist tells us even she crosses her fingers before she reads radiology reports. Surprised she's as nervous as we are, we tip our heads the way we did when she told us that not all parents get their child to every scheduled chemo.

Back then, at the beginning, wanting gold stars for timeliness, we asked, *Maybe showing up for treatments will keep us in the good stats?* As if following directions could be enough.

But the oncologist said, *No, you can't always tell. There are prognostic factors, but . . .*

Yes, but.

Odds have some meaning,
but some meaning isn't all meaning.
In this case, some meaning isn't any meaning at all.

At this appointment I ask,
Her hair is coming back and chemo is not even over, are you sure it's working?

because a woman in the grocery store told me her sister died of cancer and she knew it was going to happen because her sister's hair didn't fall out all the way.

The oncologist is used to questions like this from the parents.

She says, *This is everything we can do.*

Yes, she's sure. She looks directly into my eyes and then into your eyes.

We are doing everything we can do.

Sighing, she says, *Even I don't like scan days.* She's afraid too. She's afraid to take off work because another doctor may have to give bad news or a family might have to hear it from a doctor they don't know.

Today, good news, tempered with fear.

The oncologist's fear: we are doing everything we can do.

Our fear: we are doing everything we can do.

Chicago Gothic

for my great-grandmother

All stockyard and iron. No white picket fences, no battles. And the fire
that burnt everything clean. DuSable set up on the bend of the right river,
and things stuck: a house, some trade, a vague stink in the air, and a city
accumulated in the eddy's swirl.

I can tell that part.

But when I get to the crazy aunt who killed my great-grandmother by
pushing her down the stairs, it turns to tin.

My mother tells me at the hospital her grandmother tried to speak.
Instead, her daughter shoved a banana in her mouth to silence her, while
her grandchildren stood watching just as they had when she tumbled
down the stairs.

Fifty years later, my mother laughs—all roof of the mouth and nose.
Word choice—ge-ag, he-and, ae-nt. Two-syllable short *a* dragging detail
along to make a story for me.

For my great-grandmother, death, sweet mush, grown somewhere warm
and very far away.

Canzone Basking in the Pre-Apocalypse

for Art Bell

He tells me, "Once in awhile things happen as they did in the beginning:
chemicals fuse into suns and planets, dirt swirls out of a mist. In times
like these, we all wait for change." Once, years ago, fish grew legs and began
to creep along the shores. At this moment a different beginning,
according to the host on late night talk radio: it's all quickening,
speeding toward the moment our end will begin.
Not for all, he reassures, just for eighty percent of us. He has begun
to make plans, he says, in the 3:00 a.m. dark. His desert
home stocked, water, cans of soup, a grocery invading the deserted
sand. I listen, muscles sinking into the sheets. I begin
to sleep in the early morning, dreaming so near sleep's end
that my eyelids turn transparent and open before the dream ends.

I dream of my mother, dream a dream from her childhood: a river unending,
full of bodies floating facedown. Monkeys perch on the bodies, which are beginning
already to rot. The monkeys screech, pound their pebbly fists, pull the ends
of the long hair of the dead. They lift faces from the water, ending
their bloated sleep, waking them. My mother screams. One time,
when I was a child, she told me this dream. I want it to end.
Instead I dream: the monkeys, the river, the screeching. Nothing will end.
I see my mother on the shore. Her scream echoes. It quickens:
the bodies float faster, the monkeys screech louder, their fists fly, quickening
themselves into mallets. The dead, their drums. At once the pounding ends.
The river quiets. My mother quiets. Then she deserts
the shoreline, and I awake, alone. Again, the radio. The voice from the desert.

This time the voice is a caller who says she lives far from the desert
in the north. She knows nothing of sand and warms only at winter's end.
They talk, after my dream, as they did during, about the future: the desert,
how he will be safer there. The aliens, how they will help the deserted
few, those of us who will remain. Their fear sings me to sleep. It began
months ago when he played a tape of a screaming sasquatch. I deserted
sleep, stayed up and listened, imagining the flat desert,

the host's home, his neat cans of food and clean bottled water, time
zones away. Fluid and calm, his voice well timed,
the host calls us to call in. Wringing our hands and waiting out ends, we desert
our minds, cast bones, look to the skies for the quickening
signs. Listen. Will it sound like the monkeys, only closer, pounding more
      quickly?

Will it be dark, fiery, fluid? Will it be silent? Questions quicken
my dreams. In the dark, someone answers a phone. The voice from the desert
hisses and pops. I hear the days left in the calendar quicken.
Skiing the empty trails with the dog whose feet are quick
to leave me behind, I notice the sky, billowing red, ending
the winter day early, peeling off seconds of light. Daylight is quick
to abandon us. Iced in red light, I stare. The dog notices, slows his quick
pace, stops, and stares at me, his own red sky. Nervous, he begins
to shift his feet, whine, calling me to come, but I am still, beginning
to freeze in the darkening air. I lean toward the quickly
deepening sky. Will it split, rain spacecraft and wrath? My breath times
the seconds until the sun sets. I settle my mind. Music on the snow, my poles
      beat out sharp time.

I think I am too easily influenced, crazy, obsessed, touched, even mad. Sometimes,
I hear the minutes crunching by. Evenly at first, then quickening
into the voices, the smooth bass of the host, the crackling phone lines. At times
I imagine the gray empty of after, but then I find we are all up late, timing
the minutes. Every compass pointing south toward the desert
in the early dawn, we wait for destruction. Paranoia seasoned with ticking time,
soup boiled out of story and dread. Even we will burn off in time.
No radio. No host. No callers. Until then worry without end,
but Jesus will stand us up. No aliens will appear. The end
is actually anywhere but near. I know, but I listen all the time,
to a man taking calls, and arguing about the beginning
of the end. Believing nothing, I breathe, begin

to see that once in a while things do happen as they did in the beginning:
fear swirls out of the mist, forms suns and planets. Without us, time
looks at his watch and brushes past, and shuffling, then running, years quicken
past our doors. I need the man with the microphone in the desert,
his mad timbre, troubled dreams, because I, unlike time, will end.

The Previously Unmentioned Father

She told the children the cat went to Florida to visit his father,

but she had found him in the neighbor's yard, one leg sticking out from under the shade-loving hostas. The not-so-shade-loving cat shouldn't have been there. So when she scooped his body up, limp like a bunched orange beach towel, she wondered what she would say. What was a better place? How to introduce heaven to kids who had been to Mass once when their grandmother died, and then the oldest asked, pointing at the priest, "Is that God?"

Three days later when the kids noticed the cat still hadn't shown, she brought up Florida. And they seemed to buy it all: the previously unmentioned father, the sun, and the sandy beach.

Remembering the Day
Our Daughter Drew Your Portrait

1.

At three, our youngest
drew you, titled it:
Daddy Yelling "Knock It Off Guys!"

Lopsided, garbled precision. Left eye,
an angry swirl threatening
to swallow your face.

Three hairs. One
bent like an antenna.
Accurate portrait, I thought.

Your foul mood:
the need for a nap,
Seasonal Affective Disorder,
work stress.

Who pays attention to washable
marker other than to scrub it
from stained hands at dinner time?

The next day the hospital printer
would spit a string of sticky labels,
so long the nurse joked
If you weren't already anemic,
you're going to be
as she pressed them onto vials.

The next day your life would shift:
from bad mood
to bone marrow biopsy
and mine would grind into

the crush of your grip
as the needle hit bone,

but that night
despite my laughter,
you were not happy
with the picture she drew of you.

2.

Remember when
the receptionist, giving directions, said:
Don't freak out. The sign says
Cancer Center.

Remember the oncologist saying
I don't usually get to cure people.
A joy so rare he kept you
as his patient until
your regular doctor called him,
insisting he release
you back to her. He confessed
I'm in trouble with her
on the day you last visited him.

And when you saw her again,
she said, *Yes, definitely rare.*
Only old ladies get pernicious anemia
and prescribed a vitamin shot
that would keep you alive.

Remember the buzz of the near miss,
the wash of relief, the way the summer sun
in the parking lot that day
pulsed through our bones
as if we had no flesh between us
and the everything that isn't us:
the silver glint of light on metal,
the turning leaves,
the new dirt smell of spring,
and our daughters, their hair
blowing back as they ran laughing.

3.

On the day our daughter
drew you yelling,
I laughed. You grumped.

We didn't know to be afraid.

And the next day when we were afraid
we were afraid of the wrong thing.

By the time she was nine,
we knew new things:

     There is a play-sized MRI machine
     in the Children's Hospital
     and dolls for demonstrations.

     Social workers use teddy bears
     with chemo ports to explain

to a child what the surgeon
is going to do.

Oncologists consider a cancer
that strikes five hundred children
in this country each year
common.

Draw my portrait today:

a clenched fist
made of glass, teetering
on the edge of a table.

Leave it untitled.

On the Way to Kuyilapalayam Higher Secondary School, Puducherry, India

The teacher bus picks me up at the side of the road. Stepping up three school bus steps, the Bollywood bass and empty seats strike me. *Sit in the front*, I'm told, *You're a guest of the school.* Lurching through morning traffic, scramble of scooters and autorickshaws, we pick up teachers. Women and more women, climbing off the back of motorcycles driven by men. Women in saris so many different colors the bus blooms with each stop. We pick up a fifty-pound bag of rice, a box of something hefted on with the help of someone waiting for another bus. From the highway, the sea and the sun seem dull compared to the thump and glow of the bus on the way to school.

Tomorrow, I want to ride the student bus, seats filled with girls or boys, all matched: uniforms, polished shoes, silver tiffin boxes, braids so long they're folded over on themselves and tied with blue ribbon. I want it to be someone's birthday, the day a student can come in their own clothes with a basket of sweets to share. I want that music, to see the sun coming up over the bay to that bass. I want to take notes on the difference.

A Matter of Fact

for David Crouse

The bird's small mind has no space for the tangle of curtains or solidity
of glass. It has only one room, a minute gallery, moments framed on the
white walls: two greenish eggs in a nest built in roots, grass gone to seed.
Here, a marble bust of an ant. There, a portrait of menace in yellow eyes.
In the cat's mind there's a black door with a frosted window, backlit stencil
reading "private." Inside, a single metal chair, a bare bulb swinging from
the ceiling on a black cord. The cat knows how this is going to end, but
I don't. That's why I scramble to gather the bird off the living room floor,
even though its wing doesn't look right. I tell myself it needs quiet. I tell
the cat, *Don't kill birds.* He blinks his yellow blink. He doesn't tell himself
anything. In the morning, he drags the dead junco back into the kitchen.
Muttering and reeling, I sweep while feathers resist sweeping, floating just
in front of the dust pan for a second before renewing their flight.

Pluck the Strings without Delay

Just start the funeral now.
Today. Before any one
of us has died. Call dinner
a wake. Put some flowers
in the entry and polish
the shoes. There's a rosary
somewhere. Find it. We will
take turns lying on the table.
Hush voices, stifle smiles,
shrug, recall. Preheat
the oven. Put the dishes
on the counter. I'll pour
the wine. Go ahead sob.
I'll hold you, pat
your back. When it
happens, we will
be ready. We can say,
Oh, not this
again. And so soon.

2

For the Sake of Argument

Necessary Premises

Find two or three statements,
either true or false, to prop up the claim,
also true or false. Sort. Two boxes: True
or False. Yes or No. Keep or Throw.
Open the closet crammed
with grandfather's pants unworn
these ten years. Bring out
the attic's ruined instruments,
moldy books. Drag
soggy cardboard up the stairs.
Let the figurines clatter on the couch,
clutching each other. Keep only a few.
Or better none.
Polish the floors.
Watch squares of sun drift
across the dining room all morning.
Base everything on them.

Incomprehensible Poem

Sound, both harsh and sweet and something about fruit. That's what you've gotten so far, but you're only halfway though. Something in another language—two lines, no more. Something with a line though the O. You sound it out. The wind shifts. Bellowing. Something about sewing scissors. A cloth cut on the bias. Something broken followed by a color. *Try harder,* you think. The fricatives nod their agreement. The little slashed Os stare back heavy-lidded from the page.

Lyric Confesses

I don't like to talk about it, to go into too much detail, but sometimes
I want the engine to pull me through, through the town, through the
tunnel to the next station, smoke pounding up like a fist in the air, so
certain. I know impulse—the first wasp's breath against graying flesh,
that moment between the bud and the leaf. But at even a mention of
what comes next, I balk like the almost-sleeper startled awake. I see
the cracked ceiling, the shadow the antique light traces—a tear-like
drop stretching toward my pillow. Outside a lone voice sings, stumbling
home from the bar. I know there is a streetlight, a wrought iron bench, a
newspaper rumpled in the gutter, but I will not pull the curtain to look.

A Small, Muscular Poem

—so false it smells of fish
drowning the circus

Unusual because of its squatness,
it begins with an epigraph you
suspect might be made up, but
you don't care enough to check.
You skim, flip the page instead,
then surprise yourself as the paper
cuts you, a red split tracing
the edge of your thumb.

A Reply to the Obtrusive Narrator

Yesterday I left a marginalia of fingerprints rendered in grease. Consider them a whorled map of my heart, for I was so drawn up in your character's shame that I lost track of the crumpled napkin on my lap. Let's, for a moment, imagine that we're at the dinner party on page 312, and that I have raised my hand to my lips to be sure that no one overhears my earnest confession. After I speak, I'll smile and look down, wringing the fine linen napkin in my lap. Forgive my intrusion. Take my confidence for what it is, reaching, pregnant with longing.

Day Job

Assume, for the sake of argument,
that the desperation hasn't seeped
into Sunday night, swallowing dinner,
the table, the round Hopperesque light
in which your wife, in her best 1950s
cone bra, raises the fork to her mouth,
and that your own sadness doesn't sit
in the chair next to you, invisible, but
for a slight difference in the brushstroke,
a not-shadow on the wall that can't be seen
in the gallery, but that the viewer senses anyway.
Let's assume that the world isn't
intense pastel infused with grit and fluorescence,
and that as you crease this week's pay stub
into your palm, you don't think of the word *stub*
as the secret name for your heart.

Another Incomprehensible Poem

This one you almost recognize, but you waver. No water, no pond, murky nor crystalline. If it's only sound, it hacks and gulps. Neologistic spasms of the tongue. A tongue. Of course, always a tongue. Maybe something vague and stiff too. You get it, but the joke comes to you a beat too late and your tardy smile appears forced, showing too much gum. Your tardy smile becomes the last line.

The Loaded Question

I'm not direct.
Not snub-nosed.
Not notched.
My mother called my features
delicate, curvy,
but they pitch me as a shot.
I understand. I'm abrupt,
that's true, and there is a response,
I suppose. A blush, fresh fluster,
perhaps even a stammer.
Sometimes the eyes turn up and to the left.
Sometimes the pause is a little too long.
In that second, everyone knows. Or thinks
they know. Critics crowd,
croaking before the victim has fallen.
But he hasn't. He doesn't
stagger back clutching his chest and crumple.

If he does fall, it's slow, like an old tree
hollowed by rot. Nothing topples.
In my dream, I stand by the roadside,
pointing, but no one follows.
I am a sign, weathered, paint chipping,
an arrow flashing, fading
in the predawn light.
Detour. Detour. Detour.

Prizewinning Incomprehensible Poem

You are as surprised as the poet. Your mouth an O, mimicking the curve
of her mouth's small o as she reads, her head a moonrise above the mic.
She never says slop bucket, shift, or winter. She never says hair, groan, or
rinse water. Silver she says twice. Glass, four times. *Water can be mended,*
she insists, smiling. Her mouth almost a U, but not quite. Your mouth, a
line, an em dash. When she says *just one more,* fold your arms, nod, and
whisper *yes.*

Because This Is Not a Novel

You do not get to be the protagonist.
Drop that. Frame yourself as a figure
in the background, shadowed.
Think side dish, accompaniment.
You are that friend, the one who disappears
after the biopsy results, the one
who says she'll be there and isn't.

Maybe you have broken someone's heart.
It still hurts when they think of you.
You never even think of them.
Maybe that's you buried in the basement,
an answer to someone else's question.
Or you curled on the bed under
the pilly blue blanket
hoping he doesn't come home drunk.
You are a character actor. You were in something,
but no one knows what.

Imagine a country
where the letters squirm
and the streets darken at night
while the air fills
with insect buzz and frog chirps.
A man sees you
standing alone on the street.
But do not forget
it's not even about you then.
It's about the man,
watching through the parted curtain,
his calloused hand on the lace.
He pauses just before
he drops it back and wonders
what you're doing alone
so late at night.

Poem with Possibly Misconstrued Scientific Terms

When the poet says *geomorphic cryosphere,*
you relax thinking *at least it's not physics again,*
but after three lines this poem needs a glossary.

Umweldt and *aufeis.*

Imagine the frustrated scientist
at the residency taking another deep breath
before starting an explanation again.

Train your eyes on the poet
with the blank stare you learned
while not paying attention in right field,
Remember Big League Chew,
how you'd sit on the bleachers
shoving pinch after pinch
into your mouth until
your cheek was so swollen
with sweet gumclot
nothing you said
made sense.

Incomprehensible Manifesto

Eschew story, the stepped stair, the stringer.
Reject thread.
               Leave

the knot off the end. Pull it all
the way through. Throw the thimble

across the room. Be neither armor
nor vulnerable finger.

                       Forget confession,

cone of light, gray table.

Glare at the good cop.

                     Smile at the bad one.

Reject without object, all objects.

Offer
               a tray of vowels.
Os for dipping, Us filled with wine.

Say no thank you.

Say thank you, no. Say you thank no.

Never stir.

Break the tiny plastic swords
in half and leave them
in a pile on the bar.

Always shake.

Construct for hours. Leave bones. Leave
pants on the floor, crumpled.

The audience understands,

even applauds,
rhythmless thwacks
from the corners of the darkened room.

3

They All Came Before You

The Other Side in April

It's not greener. Admit it.
Muddy, punctuated
with burned spots
from the dogs.
Over the fence, familiar,
the other side lies.

Stand on tiptoe.

This late
spring
snow clings
to the fence posts
and paced paths,
months of boot prints
that won't melt
until May.

It's all the same,
persistent
unmelting.
In every yard,
a playhouse
buckling
under the pressure.

Explication

1.

I spoke to John Haines only once. Unlike the many Alaskan artists and writers whose paths crossed with Haines, I wasn't his student. I wasn't invited to kick my feet up in front of his woodstove at the cabin on the Richardson. We never drank together. By the time I showed up, he hadn't lived at the cabin for years. I arrived in Interior Alaska just in time to feel the shade of his shadow.

It was morning. Winter of course, and yes, thirty below. An appropriate setting for a Haines sighting. To see the poet of *Winter News* in winter is correct. But that was the only correct thing.

I was standing in the lobby of the Mary Siah Rec Center, wet-headed and barefoot, when I saw him shuffle in toward the check-in window to show his hot tub punch card to the teenaged attendant.

No fire. No woodstove. No candle. No lantern light. The lobby of the public pool is too humid for a parka, so I was in a T-shirt and he was rapidly unzipping his coat, transitioning from the frozen to liquid world.

The parents-and-tots swim class had just ended, and my daughters, one and three, wilded with the crowd of toddlers on the foam patchwork tiles under the Little Tykes plastic picnic table. Screeching and crawling and wet-haired crazy. What must it have seemed like to Haines and the crowd of elderly men arriving for their weekly Sourdough hot tubbing session? Fairbanks toddlers spinning and dropping goldfish crackers in orange trails behind them, so unlike the ghostly newsboys making the rounds. Unfrozen and pink from the hot showers, they slaughtered the morning's silence with their joy.

I had seen him at the pool the week before and the week before that, but I was too intimidated to say anything. *That's John-fucking-Haines*, I'd think as I crammed small boots onto small feet while our car warmed up. *He's going into the hot tub*, I'd think as I crawled around on the floor picking up crushed crackers. The sign on the wall reminded parents it was our responsibility to clean up after snacks.

I was a poet too, or thought so, and also unable to speak, my mouth framed on a stifled *Hello, Mr. Haines* . . . so each week, without a sound from me, he passed into the steam of the men's locker room, leaving his boots in the cubbies on his way to the tub.

But this day, maybe because his age seemed another door about to open and shut behind him, one that I wasn't going to be allowed to pass through, I said something. I went up, disheveled, wet hair, leaking milk from one nipple, and said, *Mr. Haines, thank you for your poems*. He didn't hear me, of course. He didn't hear well by then. I repeated myself, loudly and into his ear. Flattered, he asked *Which one?* But stupidly all I could manage to say was *All of them*.

And I was lying.

Seascape with Eagle, Driftwood, Ravens, Seagull, Two Men, and Their Phones

The ravens look miniature compared to the eagle crouched in the crook of a driftwood tree, tearing a seagull to shreds.

Think beach bone, skeleton perch. Think rock, tide-worn.

The man I watch watches the eagle, ignoring the ravens and the breeze at the back of his neck until he can't, and pulls his hoodie over his ears, moves closer, stalking, like the ravens. The eagle ignores them both.

Think caw and clatter. Think dumpster kings, menacing syrupy sound.

Unnoticed, I notice the man, who notices only the eagle; and the ravens, who notice only the eagle and the seagull; and the eagle, who notices only the wind and the seagull, who, being dead, notices nothing.

Think eyeball and red strip. Think rib cage and beak.

Then another man, beach walking, notices everything—first man, ravens, eagle, seagull—except me.

Think tentative shiver and stilt, shrugged shoulders and slight lean.

Facing each other across the driftwood, the men take out their phones, aim at the eagle and at each other, kneel, praying, *just stay still*, holding their breath to steady whatever quivers inside them that I can't see.

Think virtual click. Think definitive proof.

Is the eagle even in the picture I took of two men taking pictures of an eagle and each other taking pictures of an eagle with their phones?

Think two-toned, sidelong. Think feathered indifference. Think abstraction. Think stare.

The seagull was there. I have proof. After the men moved on, after the ravens moved on, the eagle flew, a wisp of sound over the lapping waves. In its talons hung the seagull's ragged flesh, one feather dangling, an inverted flag claiming the small country to which it clung. No one took a picture of it.

Picking Cranberries

The week after you arrived, I took you
cranberry picking
on the trails close to town.
You told me

about your husband, your clenched jaw,
the damage the pressure had done.
I picked, fingers pulling, cooling
against hard, dark berries.

Buckets filled, sun slanted
through the birch. That afternoon
our words puffed visible
from our mouths, and I knew what

it had been for you, arriving more
difficult than departing. I reached
for your bucket and poured in my berries.
I can see you

in your kitchen in December, the short day
peers in the window while your hands
break open the bag. One square of pale
sunlight on the sugar, measured, waiting.

Vernal Equinox

There is no halfway here,
even though it's halfway to summer, even
though the sun is halfway along
its path, which is your path too,
the one on the ridge that passes the sheep
chewing with their tear and crunch
the only sound of the noonday,
except for your boots, which grind
along the trail, sometimes rock
swept clean of snow, sometimes
ice, left from the odd melt in December,
the one that pushed cars into ditches,
flipped the school bus
and surprised you—so warm so
soon, so long before the light.

Explication

2.

I have a broadside signed by Haines of "Poem of the Forgotten." Years ago, shortly after Haines's death, I bid on it in a silent auction and won.

I'm not entirely happy about owning it. Haines may loom large on the Interior Alaskan literary landscape, but in my house that broadside hangs in the back corner of the basement, tucked away on a wall just in front of the gun safe.

The poem irritates me. Haines's confidence, his certainty that he belonged in Alaska and that Alaska belonged to him makes me narrow my eyes and shake my head. *Who gets to feel that way?* I ask, but only inside my head.

I don't use the gun safe often, so I don't have to look at the poem too much. I don't know why I framed it. Maybe it was the crabbed signature. A feeling of obligation? It's a signed broadside by John-fucking-Haines, after all.

Here in Interior Alaska, the poets all knew Haines. They have stories, mostly reverent. They shake their heads appreciatively, smile. Sometimes they acknowledge how damn difficult he could be. Some still have their hackles up over his own famous hackles. Most seem to see him through a haze, imagining themselves each the silent owl, sitting beside him in a shadowy spruce, with a drifting moon and a muttering river nearby.

I can't even imagine flying beside Haines, looking down on the snow. In my mind he's always floating, above or beyond, toward Asia, or somewhere else so far from the reality of my family-tethered Alaska life that I have to hold my hand up to shade my eyes when I look for him.

I do have to look at the broadside occasionally. On the other side of the drywall behind it is the nook under the stairs where I stash a pile

of Capri Suns and granola bars I bought on sale at Costco. Snacks
for swim practice, a duty I undertake to fulfill my required parental
volunteer hours, so I can avoid paying additional fees to my now-teenaged
daughter's swim team.

I still see Haines because of swimming.

Maybe I framed it out of respect for my own hackles. Some Saturday
mornings, bending to fill a canvas bag with snacks, I reread the poem
and think to myself, *That arrogant attitude toward nature is why the world's
ending*, shake my head, and then try to go on with my life.

It's Possible the Mountain Doesn't Exist

for my uncle Bobby

They're going to tell you the gray obscures a mountain. The largest one
in North America. They're going to tell you a height. Statistics. Granite.
Basalt. They're going to tell you four guys walked up it with some rope
and a bag of donuts in 1913. They're going to tell you this was crazy.

You're going to think they're crazy. There's no mountain. Only gray
clouds, only words describing a mountain printed on a platform designed
for you to see a mountain that you cannot see today.

It's there. It's been there. It's definitely there. Believe us, they say, it's
beautiful.

You will begin to suspect the Glade Mountain Fresh can you saw in the
bathroom on the train from which you could also not see the mountain is
part of a scam.

Don't worry, even if you saw it, your camera would have shrunk it. And
when you showed the photo to your friends back home, you'd say *It looks
bigger than this.*

Believe me, you would have been disappointed. Almost as disappointed
as you are right now.

Afternoon Light

Slant, slide down
the ridges and slopes
make shadows look so good
people forget the coming night,
the twenty-degree temperature drop.
Make them want to take a photograph
and fail. Photos can't catch
the dropped jaw, the breath's sharp draw.

Exist then disappear.

Remind them that despite the snow,
the arcs of white, despite shadowy ridges,
despite the sad thermometer,
despite crystallized breath,
nothing is ever frozen.

Make them see that under three feet of ice
water flows, unstilled, but don't ever
give them proof you were there.

Explication

3.

As a poet I was born in a particular place, a hillside overlooking the Tanana River in central Alaska, where I built a house and lived for the better part of twenty-two years.
—John Haines

Haines came to Alaska as a transplant, like me. But we're not the same. My arrival in Alaska in 1994 coincided with him leaving after his storied battle to get an appointment at an Alaskan university ended in failure. He was packing his frustrations and heading south just as I drove a loaded Honda Accord up the highway. I came up to work on an MFA, a degree Haines didn't believe was particularly useful.

I lived in a dry cabin for years, but it was in town. Hauling water involved a trip to the laundromat instead of the river. The post-pipeline Alaska I landed in was not the Homestead-Act Alaska Haines came to in 1947.

During my early years in Fairbanks, I only saw him from a seat in the audience at readings he occasionally gave with the local arts association. He seemed distant, his fame cloudlike—changing the color of whatever he floated over. Haines's poems work toward the mythic layers of humanness. I was twenty-something, a poet from Outside, I felt an obligation to admire his work.

Haines believed that when a poet lived alone in the woods "an older consciousness of nature, overgrown by education, slowly begins to reassert itself."

As if the only way for us to see our true-true selves is to walk away from each other.

Picking Crowberries

Late this fall we pick crowberries
because the blueberries had gone,
skins split from frost, wrinkled purple.

You pulled branches up, hoping,
but we had come too late.
The crowberries, hang low on moss,
still firm. We settle for them,

too seedy for anything but syrup.
I kneel by the plank path and reach
for piney stalks. I am the new arrival,
dropped in the woods with you.

My fingers feel newly attached, spindly, clean.
Yours feel certain. As I drop the first handful,
they bounce across the bottom of the bucket.

At the truck stop, the waitress
sees our stained hands, smiles, "Berries?"
"Yes," we say, forks poised above pie,
ready to break the crust.

Winter Landscape with Flirting Tourists

On the Savage River where overflow
crackles underfoot,
the couple, so bundled
they seem synthetic,
shouts, packs failed snowballs
out of too-dry snow.

I want to say,
That doesn't work here,
but who am I
not to let someone find out on their own,
so I pass them on the trail,
jean jacket and bare hands
because who are they
to define cold.

And who am I to define at all.
They have the words,
bright syllables built
of the pull between them.
I have only the trail's styrene crunch
and the hush of exhalation.

I take a picture of a rock,
of wind-scalloped snow,
each rise molded,
while they take a picture
of the hazy mountain.
They walk the frozen river
in the opposite direction.

I come back in the quiet,
past the trailhead,
past their rental car,

while the mouthless trees
inch closer,
unable to call my name.

Explication

4.

Does wilderness, in the isolated form that Haines depends on, even really exist? Does emptiness? Richardson wasn't empty when he arrived. It just looked empty to him.

Haines wasn't alone much of the time at Richardson. He acknowledged it, writing, "There is one part of it I have hardly mentioned and that concerns the two women who lived there much of the time, and one in particular." The vaguest of mention, no names, no description.

And even in his constructed "aloneness" he courted an epistolary relationship with very famous poets Outside who became the champions of his work.

My painter friend, Kes, told me, *You have a problem with nature writing.* And yes, I do. Writing that posits the single self in the wilderness as the key to enlightenment irritates me. We aren't trapped into solitary pursuit of the "older consciousness." There must be other passages between "the lines between human and animal" that don't depend on transplanting oneself onto a faux-empty land.

Other passages. No one is ever actually alone.

The Word I Will Not Use about the Wolf

I saw the alpha female walk down the road with the sheep leg in her mouth. I will not pretend we were not in the car even though in the picture you can't tell we were in the white Subaru on the dirt road. I saw the alpha female walk down the road past a line of cars, past hand after hand, holding phones out the windows. I will not pretend that I knew what was in her mouth. I thought it was a ptarmigan, forgetting that in September, the ptarmigan would not be white. My eyes knew flesh, even torn, despite bald spots, hide hanging, which I took for feathers. Collared, tracked, plotted in bits and numbers, statistically analyzed, even her scat gathered in plastic bags turned over for scrutiny, her tracks filled with plaster, preserved in the visitor center shouting *please touch me*, she was never alone. Not the kind of *alone* we imagine. And I was as unalone too. I watched the wolf while I was wearing a seatbelt in the passenger seat. Casual, she padded beside the still cars on the road in front of the mountain. September, bright blue and hot. We sat until she was not in our rearview. Later the ranger told us she came to her den in the tundra and the pups ran out and ate, howling small howls in celebration while the cars, stilled and shut off sat rocklike in the road. She didn't care. She didn't look toward the cars. She didn't feel our need for her to be real, as real as the sunlight pounding through our windshields, as real as the ragged tooth of the big mountain so clear in front of us. That was the road we were on. She was a wolf. A park wolf. Important wolf. Alpha wolf. I remember another alpha female trapped just outside the park boundary a few years before. A Toklat wolf. Important wolf. The last of a particular beautiful, like the crisp September sun before the mute dark of winter. I will not use the word mourn. None of us who sat and watched deserves it.

Explication

5.

No one taught me to give birth. My body just did it. Nature, wilderness, place, instinct, it was always there inside me. The exact knowing what to do. The particular grunt right at the beginning of pushing. It doesn't matter that her fist was up in a Supergirl salute. I figured it out not because I had to, which I did, but because I already knew what to do. Like all the women before me. Like all the mammals before me.

Nature appears in the body, in relation to other people—one person who was being born, others who were trying to help me survive that birth. The birth I almost didn't survive. Or I only survived because they helped me.

Even in almost not-living my body knew what it had to do, and if it had to die for the baby it would have. I did not have to go somewhere alone, depart, cut ties, build a house, and listen to owls to learn this. I just knew.

Haines posits wilderness as a single door through which only one soul can pass.

Living in Fairbanks, I can see Haines's door every day. Wilderness, yes: moose in the garden, a green-and-purple aurora, the crunch of snowshoes at twenty below.

There are other doors. Even some we contain.

A Song for Forgetting

—after John Haines

1.

Unlike you, I can't touch the moment I
saw myself as self first. I don't know when I came
into the sense that I was alone, built of thoughts too
scattered to whisper, *right here, only this,*
I never believed that anywhere anyplace,
owed me anything, not explanation, not a
definition. You see, young
women don't get to define "human,"
at least not the way the oldest spruce, green
despite the white and
dark, gets to define lonely.

2.

I could tell myself I was sick of the world or well
acquainted with it. I could begin once more or quit,
walk off onto the spring ice. A choice built of
years of waiting, of the not-yet-green inside, the
fireweed, knotty buds timing the end of the world.

3.

Every line ends with I
because you begin there, with you framed
against a wildness you painted a
dark blue. Each brushstroke a house
built of hair and pigment, built of
peeled spruce, built of silence and moss.
You don't seem to believe in the word *and,*
instead you take stock in splitting wood, in timber,
stacked for yourself against the coming dark. You called
that silence. Is that it?
The soundless music of a
man who tried to build his breath into a home?

4.

I want to abandon *I*,
make something that can be made
my own despite me, reconstruct shards of my
bed, that summer sweat and tangled-blanket bed,
where the darkness pools, under
sunlight as it falls on the quilt. The
hidden shadow, the shadow
of cold, trembles in fear of
leaves budding, waiting until light leaves
and strips the trees skeletal and
bone-bleached. Imagine holding a wake
in the hours before death, in
the days before the
first day you'll spend alone. In the first
snow, your footprints (a line that says *now,*
of course, now) on top of the language of
autumn leaves gone gold. Autumn
and its contractions, each lost second of light filed
away, unread. Don't chatter. You'll have more luck with
winter's language. Learn to speak in silences.

5.

Because no one can point to when
breath leaves the body, we
can't say that we know
anything but the hum there
outside the window. The light is
ribboned across the blankets on the bed, no
sunset yet, just another gold line, upon one
more, upon another. From folded hands to
soles, all light and quiet, nothing left to hear.

Winter, Moving Still

You want to believe nothing
stays awake through the freeze.
But you, who need a coat,

a cabin, a fire burning
in the stove, down
bag and pillow,

you're the one who burns
something else to survive.

Ask why.

Your answer, an accounting
of small things: vole tracks,
rose galls, frost-shriveled berries

still on the branch, crunch of snow,
ice-crackle, the shush of a sheep's jaw
chewing the last browned grass.

Your stolen,
illuminated breath clouds
the cone of headlamp.

Put out the lantern,
let the stove-tick
sing you to sleep.

Its song is younger than the owl's,
who is younger yet than moonlight
and the shifting lights in the sky.

They all came before you,
and while you sleep,
eyes closed, they keep
always moving.

Notes

"Explication 3"
The epigraph is from John Haines's essay "The Writer as Alaskan: Beginnings and Reflections," which I first read in *Living Off the Country: Essays in Poetry and Place*. It has been widely quoted and reprinted in other places as well. His biographers seem fond of quoting various parts of this essay.

"Explication 4"
The quote from Haines in this piece also comes from "The Writer as Alaskan: Beginnings and Reflections" in *Living off the Country: Essays in Poetry and Place*.

"A Song for Forgetting"
This poem is a golden shovel that incorporates John Haines's "Poem of the Forgotten," the text of which I took directly from the broadside that hangs near my gun safe. I am indebted to Terrance Hayes, who invented the golden shovel as a form in response to Gwendolyn Brooks's poem "We Real Cool." I first read "Poem of the Forgotten" in Haines's *News from the Glacier* the first year I arrived in Alaska. The poem has lived many lives beyond books and the broadside. John Luther Adams set "Poem of the Forgotten" to music in 2004, and in 2013 the Alaska State Council for the Arts installed the poem on a plaque near the Northfork Public Use Cabin in the Chena River Recreation Area.

Thank you to Sandra Beasly, Julie Marie Wade, Tess Taylor, Peggy Shumaker, and Joeth Zucco for reading drafts of this manuscript. Sarah Doetschman, there is nothing I can do to thank you for your careful reading and brilliant reordering. I am so fortunate to call you friend and my poems are doubly fortunate to have you as an editor. With love and gratitude to T.J. O' Donnell, for the years of presence, for being alongside for the living and the writing.